PASSERS AND RECEIVERS

The NFL's Top Touchdown Duos

By Richard
Deutsch

*Quarterback
Mark Brunell
of the Jacksonville
Jaguars*

A SPORTS ILLUSTRATED FOR KIDS BOOK

CONTENTS

165
303

8:24

9NEWS

850 KOA
BRONCOS RADIO

Sprint

IRVIN
88

39
BRONCOS

2

Wide receiver Michael Irvin of the Dallas Cowboys takes to the air to make a leaping catch!

TOM DIPACE

INTRODUCTION

Every time an NFL quarterback takes a snap and drops back to throw the ball, he is under tremendous pressure. In a matter of seconds, he has to review many things. "What is the defense doing? How is my blocking holding up? Did I call the right play?" These are just a few of the questions a quarterback has to think about as he scans the field, looking for *someone* to throw the ball to.

A quarterback's favorite receiver is the player who can help answer those questions. It can take anywhere from several games to several years for a quarterback and a receiver to really start working well together on the field. But once they develop that connection, look out! The quarterback and his number-one receiver become more than just two members of the same team. They become a dangerous touchdown duo!

SPORTS ILLUSTRATED FOR KIDS' *Passers and Receivers* profiles seven super pairs of touchdown teammates. You'll read about all the best quarterbacks and their favorite targets! There's mighty Minnesota's Randy (Moss) and Randall (Cunningham) show, Dallas' dynamite duo of Troy Aikman and Michael Irvin, and the legendary San Francisco pair, Steve Young and Jerry Rice.

We have tons of information on all of the players, including some fun facts that even their coaches may not know. Want to find out more? Just turn the page!

Wouldn't it be cool if you could communicate with a friend without saying a word? That's what it's like for quarterback Steve Young and wide receiver Jerry Rice of the San Francisco 49ers. They know each other so well that Steve can tell Jerry what to do without even opening his mouth!

"There are times when I'm about to take the snap and I'll catch Jerry's eye to let him know what is going to happen, and off we go," says Steve.

Every time Steve and Jerry line up for a play, there's a good chance that it could go for a touchdown. Steve has been throwing to Jerry for years. In that time, the two have teamed up for a whopping 84 touchdowns. That's the most ever for a quarterback–wide receiver duo in the NFL!

"They know each other so well that Steve could probably put a blindfold on and throw some of his timing patterns to Jerry," says San Francisco head coach Steve Mariucci.

But it wasn't always so easy for Steve and Jerry. Jerry spent the first six years of his career catching passes from Joe Montana. Joe was a right-handed quarterback, and he threw soft, low passes.

Everything changed for Jerry when Steve became the starting quarterback, in 1991. Steve throws the ball hard and high. Plus, Steve is left-handed, so the ball spins differently in the air.

It was a learning experience for both players. "Steve is a totally different quarterback from Joe, so I

PLEASE TURN TO PAGE 7

"He's just having fun. He's like a little kid out there running around on the field."— Jerry Rice on Steve Young

Jerry (left) and Steve have taken the San Francisco 49ers to the top.

SCO 49ERS

STEVE YOUNG
QUARTERBACK

Steve beats defenses with his scrambling ability and accurate arm.

STEVE FACTS

BORN: October 11, 1961, in Salt Lake City, Utah
HEIGHT: 6' 2"
WEIGHT: 215 pounds
COLLEGE: Brigham Young University
ENTERED NFL: 1985
CAREER HIGHLIGHTS: Steve is the most efficient passer in NFL history.
FUN FACT: After college, Steve earned a law degree.

STEVE RATES:
10 of 10 for scrambling

TIM UMPHREY

JERRY FACTS

BORN: October 13, 1962, in
Crawford, Mississippi
HEIGHT: 6' 2"
WEIGHT: 196 pounds
COLLEGE: Mississippi Valley State
ENTERED NFL: 1985
CAREER HIGHLIGHTS: Jerry is the
NFL's all-time leading receiver.
FUN FACT: During the off-season,
Jerry runs over hills to stay
in shape.

JERRY RATES:
10 of 10 for hands

JERRY RICE
WIDE RECEIVER

> "Jerry's the guy you can count on getting open at the most crucial times."
> — Steve Young

Jerry has scored more touchdowns than any other player in NFL history!

had to throw everything out the door and say, 'Okay, this is Steve Young,' " Jerry says.

Steve had to learn to be patient. "It took a lot of time to figure out how Jerry wanted the ball and where he wanted it," Steve says.

Now, after so many seasons together, Steve knows exactly where Jerry wants the ball to be thrown. And when two great players know each other so well, they are nearly unstoppable.

Never were Steve and Jerry more super than in Super Bowl XXIX, in 1995. Steve threw for a record six touchdowns as San Francisco thrashed the San Diego Chargers, 49–26. Three of those scoring passes went to Jerry.

Jerry injured his knee badly in 1997 and missed most of the season. When he came back in 1998, nobody knew whether he would still be a great receiver.

In the first game, against the New York Jets, Jerry caught a 16-yard pass from Steve and was tackled very hard. Everyone thought he might be hurt again, but Jerry got right up and kept on playing! He finished the game with six catches for 86 yards and a touchdown.

Jerry didn't stop there. He caught 82 passes in all in 1998. He finished third in the NFC in receptions. Steve threw for 4,170 yards. He led the league with 36 touchdowns and was voted to his seventh Pro Bowl.

Says Jerry: "Steve and I have something that can put us at the top of the game."

Enough said.

BUFFALO BILLS

DOUG FLUTIE
QUARTERBACK

DEEHOOG/TDP

"We're always having fun when Doug is the quarterback."
— Eric Moulds

On the move! Doug is one of the NFL's most mobile quarterbacks.

Before the 1998 NFL season, quarterback Doug Flutie and wide receiver Eric Moulds of the Buffalo Bills played a ton of basketball together. Once the season began, it was as if they had brought their hoops game with them. Doug's passes to Eric on the football field were as dangerous as their fast breaks on the basketball court. Every pass had the potential to end in a slam-dunk score! "We played basketball almost every day," Eric says. "It really helped us bond, and it carried over to the football field."

People first started noticing Doug's alley-oops to Eric in a victory over the Carolina Panthers on October 25. Doug threw for 282 yards and Eric caught five passes for 145 yards and two touchdowns. One of those touchdowns went for 82 yards!

"Eric is just a phenomenal athlete," Doug says. "I saw it on the basketball court."

Nobody in the NFL saw much of Doug's talent until the 1998 season. Doug played in the Canadian Football League (CFL) from 1990 until 1997. He was named the league's Most Outstanding Player six times! Doug had gone to play in the CFL because most NFL teams thought he was too short to be a starting quarterback. He played for three different teams in the CFL and proved he could be a star there. But Doug still wanted to be a star in the NFL.

Before the 1998 season, Doug joined the Bills as a backup. The Bills weren't

PLEASE TURN TO PAGE 11

Doug may not have Eric's size (below, left), but the two usually see eye to eye when it comes to scoring touchdowns!

BUFFALO BILLS

TOM DiPACE

ERIC FACTS

BORN: July 17, 1973, in Lucedale, Mississippi
HEIGHT: 6'
WEIGHT: 204 pounds
COLLEGE: Mississippi State
ENTERED NFL: 1996
CAREER HIGHLIGHTS: Eric set a playoff record last year against Miami with 240 receiving yards.
FUN FACT: Eric returned four punts for touchdowns in his first five high school games.

ERIC RATES:
10 of 10 for speed

ERIC MOULDS
WIDE RECEIVER

"He's a great athlete. He's pretty phenomenal." —
Doug Flutie on Eric Moulds

supposed to win many games. They started out by losing three of their first four games. Then Doug took over at quarterback, and the Bills began winning. He threw for 2,711 yards and 20 touchdowns, and helped Buffalo stampede into the playoffs.

"Doug's a very athletic person," says Bills running back Antowain Smith. "He continues to do things that amaze his teammates."

One of Doug's most memorable plays was a pass to Eric in a big comeback triumph over the Miami Dolphins in November 1998. The Bills were losing 24–14 in the fourth quarter. They had the ball at the Miami 48. Doug needed a quick score, so he called a play for Eric.

Eric used his size and strength to get past two Miami defenders and into the open. Doug threw a perfect pass. Eric caught it at the 17 and ran into the end zone for a touchdown. Slam dunk! The Bills went on to win, 30–24.

"We needed a big play, something to spark us," says Doug. "And Eric came up with it!"

Eric made big plays all season for the Bills. He finished the year with 67 catches for 1,368 yards and nine touchdowns. "I just go out every week and try to make plays and be consistent," Eric says.

Doug and Eric made so many great plays that they were both voted to play in the Pro Bowl. Can you guess where they went when they got home?

To the nearest basketball court, of course! 🏈

Eric's speed gives him a leg up on the competition!

MARK BRUNELL
QUARTERBACK

Quarterback Mark Brunell and wide receiver Jimmy Smith of the Jacksonville Jaguars are two tough cats. Every time it looks as if injuries are going to ruin things for them, Mark and Jimmy claw their way back and do great things on the football field.

That's what happened in the AFC wild-card playoff game against the New England Patriots in January 1999. Mark had badly sprained his ankle three weeks earlier. He hadn't played in nearly a month. But Mark quickly shook off the rust once the game got underway. He threw for 161 yards and led the Jaguars to a convincing 25–10 win over the Patriots. One of Mark's throws was a perfect 37-yard touchdown pass to Jimmy.

"I couldn't have been happier to see Mark play again," says Jimmy. "And he didn't miss a beat!"

Jimmy understood what Mark had been through because he had gone through similar experiences. Jimmy had to overcome serious injuries to become one of the NFL's top receivers. He started his NFL career with the Dallas Cowboys in 1992, but he couldn't stay healthy. He broke his leg that season. The next year, he had to have emergency surgery to remove his appendix.

Jimmy missed two entire seasons after he was released by the Cowboys and the Philadelphia Eagles. Those tough times ended for Jimmy when he signed with the Jaguars, in February 1995. Since then, he has stayed healthy. He has also teamed up with Mark to put up some pretty sick numbers!

PLEASE TURN TO PAGE 14

Mark is known as a scrambler, but he is also a confident and dangerous drop-back passer.

PAUL JASIENSKI

JAGUARS

M. DEEHOOGTOP

MARK FACTS

BORN: **September 17, 1970, in Los Angeles, California**
HEIGHT: **6' 1"**
WEIGHT: **218 pounds**
COLLEGE: **University of Washington**
ENTERED NFL: **1993**
CAREER HIGHLIGHTS: **Mark was named MVP of the Pro Bowl in 1997.**
FUN FACT: **Mark is an outdoorsman who loves hunting and fishing.**

MARK RATES:
10 of 10 for leadership

"It's hard to find anyone who throws a sharper pass than Mark." — Jimmy Smith

In 1996, Jimmy's first full season as a starter, he had 83 catches and led the AFC with 1,244 receiving yards! Jimmy caught 82 passes in 1997. He hauled in another 78 passes the next season.

"I was fortunate to get a third chance to make it in the NFL," Jimmy says. "I worked hard and was determined to make it."

Mark has also made the best of *his* opportunities. He became Jacksonville's starting quarterback in 1995. Two years later, he led the AFC in passing. He has played in two Pro Bowls. Like superstar Steve Young of the San Francisco 49ers, Mark is a left-handed thrower with lots of mobility. And Mark knows how to lead his team in crunch time.

"I'm not sure how you defend against Mark," says Denver Bronco coach Mike Shanahan. "He's going to make big plays."

Coach Shanahan speaks from experience. One of the biggest plays Mark — and Jimmy — ever made was in a first-round playoff game against the Broncos in Denver in 1997. With just over three minutes left in the game, Jacksonville led the heavily favored Broncos, 23–20.

The Jaguars faced a third-and-five from the Denver 16. Mark told Jimmy to go for the corner of the end zone. Jimmy ran toward the corner and Mark threw a perfect pass for the game-winning touchdown. The victory was a huge surprise, but the pass wasn't — at least not to Jimmy.

"All I had to do was hold my arms out," Jimmy says. "It was perfect." 🏈

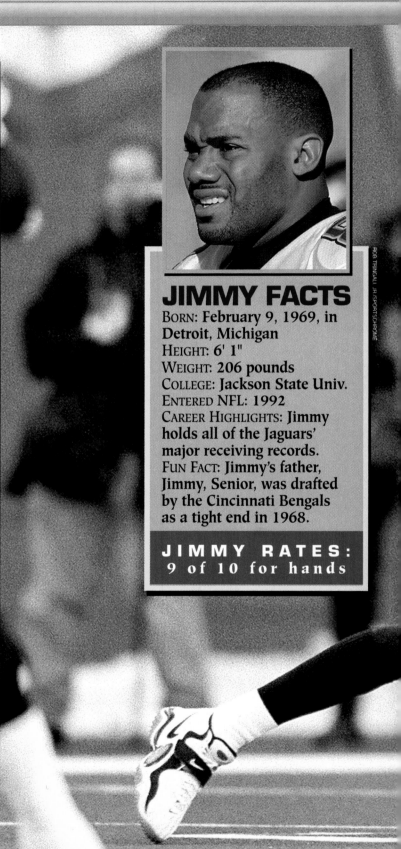

JIMMY FACTS

BORN: **February 9, 1969, in Detroit, Michigan**
HEIGHT: **6' 1"**
WEIGHT: **206 pounds**
COLLEGE: **Jackson State Univ.**
ENTERED NFL: **1992**
CAREER HIGHLIGHTS: **Jimmy holds all of the Jaguars' major receiving records.**
FUN FACT: **Jimmy's father, Jimmy, Senior, was drafted by the Cincinnati Bengals as a tight end in 1968.**

**JIMMY RATES:
9 of 10 for hands**

JAGUARS

JIMMY SMITH
WIDE RECEIVER

Jimmy uses his speed and cutting ability to get open downfield.

> "He's going to be one of the league's top receivers."
> — Mark Brunell on Jimmy Smith

15

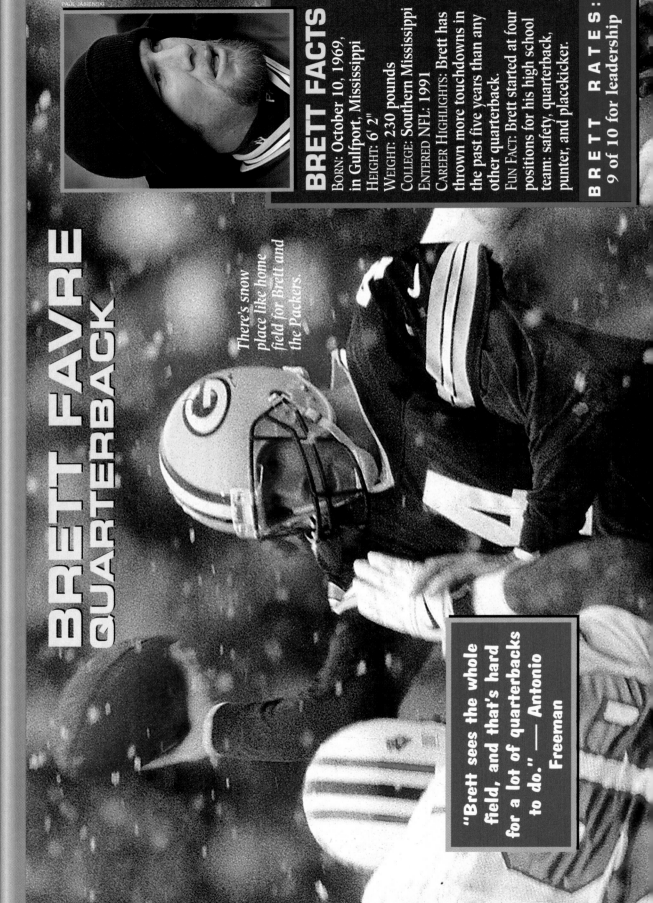

PAUL JASIENSKI

GREEN BAY PACKERS

BRETT FAVRE
QUARTERBACK

There's snow place like home field for Brett and the Packers.

BRETT FACTS

BORN: October 10, 1969, in Gulfport, Mississippi
HEIGHT: 6' 2"
WEIGHT: 230 pounds
COLLEGE: Southern Mississippi
ENTERED NFL: 1991
CAREER HIGHLIGHTS: Brett has thrown more touchdowns in the past five years than any other quarterback.
FUN FACT: Brett started at four positions for his high school team: safety, quarterback, punter, and placekicker.

BRETT RATES:
9 of 10 for leadership

"Brett sees the whole field, and that's hard for a lot of quarterbacks to do." — Antonio Freeman

DAMIAN STROHMEYER/ALLSPORT

Brett and Antonio exchange high fives during Super Bowl XXXI. Both players put up big numbers to help lead the Packers to victory.

The Green Bay Packers ruled the NFL in the 1960's and won the first two Super Bowls. After that, the Packers' magic faded. It took Green Bay 29 years to get back to the Super Bowl. How did they do it? Well, quarterback Brett Favre and wide receiver Antonio Freeman had something to do with it!

Brett has broken almost every Packer passing record. Antonio is the club's all-time leader in playoff touchdown catches. And the two have more in common than just records.

"Antonio thinks the same way as me," says Brett. "We prepare as hard as we can all week. Then on game day we just let it go."

Brett was drafted by the Falcons in 1991. In 1992, the Packers traded for Brett and made him their starting quarterback. Good move! Brett has taken the Pack to the playoffs in each of the last seven seasons. In that time, Brett has won three NFL Most Valuable Player awards!

Antonio is one of the main reasons for Brett's success. In three seasons, from 1996 through 1998, Brett threw 35 touchdown passes to Antonio. "When we get on a roll, it's hard to stop us," Brett says.

The Packers drafted Antonio in 1995. But the team wasn't sure he could succeed as a starting wide receiver. At first, they used him mostly as a punt and kick returner. This made Antonio angry.

PLEASE TURN TO PAGE 19

JOHN BIEVER/SPORTS ILLUSTRATED

GREEN BAY PACKERS

ANTONIO FREEMAN
WIDE RECEIVER

TOM DIPACE

ANTONIO FACTS

BORN: May 27, 1972, in Baltimore, Maryland
HEIGHT: 6' 1"
WEIGHT: 198 pounds
COLLEGE: Virginia Tech
ENTERED NFL: 1995
CAREER HIGHLIGHTS: Antonio has the third highest punt-return average in playoff history.
FUN FACT: Antonio once caught 10 passes while he had a cast on his left arm!

ANTONIO RATES:
8 of 10 for speed

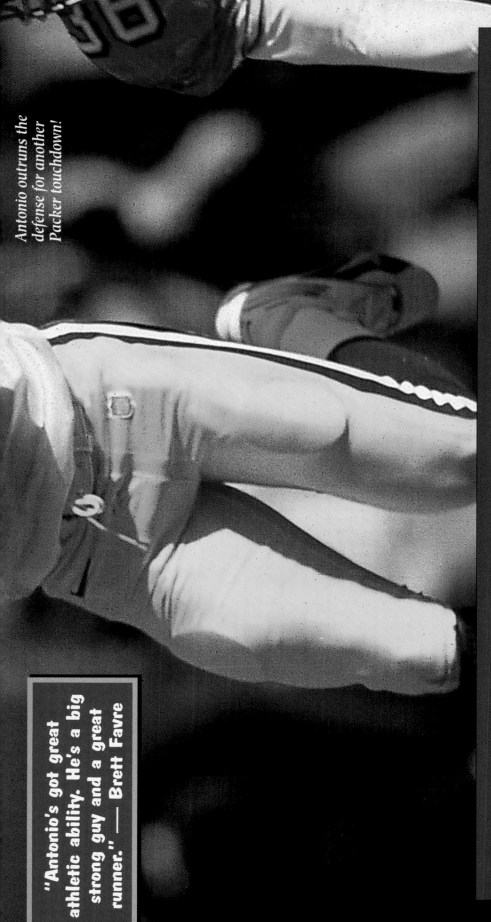

Antonio outruns the defense for another Packer touchdown!

> "Antonio's got great athletic ability. He's a big strong guy and a great runner."
> — Brett Favre

"It really lit a fire under me!" Antonio says. When Antonio did get chances to play wide receiver, he made the most of them. It didn't take him long to start burning up defenses. By 1996, Antonio was one of Brett's main targets. He caught 56 passes for 933 yards and nine touchdowns. The next season, Antonio led the Packers with 81 catches for 1,243 yards and 12 scores.

In 1998, the Pack's passing attack lit up the league. Brett's 4,212 passing yards were the most in the entire NFL. Antonio caught a career-high 84 receptions and led the league with 1,424 receiving yards.

Now everyone expects the most from Brett and Antonio. "They are as good a duo as there is in the league," says former Chicago Bear head coach Dave Wannstedt.

Brett and Antonio come up big in big games. In Super Bowl XXXI, in 1997, the Packers faced the New England Patriots. Brett and Antonio hooked up for 105 yards in the game. They also set a Super Bowl record with an 81-yard touchdown strike. The Packers won, 35–21.

In Super Bowl XXXII, in 1998, the Packers were edged by the powerful Denver Broncos, 31–24. But Brett and Antonio still put on a show. Brett hit Antonio nine times for 126 yards and two touchdowns.

What's the key to this duo's super success? It's pretty simple. "I call the plays and Antonio gets open," Brett says. "It's like he always knows where I want to go with the ball."

MINNESOTA

RANDALL CUNNINGHAM
QUARTERBACK

Thanks to quarterback Randall Cunningham and wide receiver Randy Moss, the bomb is Da' Bomb in Minnesota. Long, deep passes are known as bombs in football. And Randall and Randy have become one of the NFL's top bomb squads.

The Vikings have even invented a rule to make sure that Randall throws plenty of long passes to Randy. The rule is called the Cunningham Rule. It says that even if Randy is well-covered on a long pass play, Randall should throw the ball to him, anyway!

"You toss it deep and they either have to interfere with Randy or he will catch it," Randall says. "If he is even with a defender, then I put it up higher and let him jump."

The Vikings and their fans love the Rule. But their opponents don't. "If [a long pass] is underthrown, Moss is going to go up and catch it," says Carolina Panther cornerback Doug Evans. "If it's overthrown, he can catch up to it with his speed."

Randall and Randy picked the coolest time to show the world how well the rule works. They were playing against the mighty Green Bay Packers on *Monday Night Football* on October 5, 1998. Randall tossed two long bombs to Randy for touchdowns. The Vikes creamed the Pack, 37–24. Randall threw for 442 yards in all. Randy accounted for 190 of those yards with five catches.

"This was the greatest night in my football career," Randall said after the game. That's pretty amazing, considering that Randall is a 13-season NFL veteran.

PLEASE TURN TO PAGE 23

BOB ROSATO/SPORTS ILLUSTRATED

RANDALL FACTS
BORN: **March 27, 1963, in Santa Barbara, California**
HEIGHT: **6' 4"**
WEIGHT: **205 pounds**
COLLEGE: **University of Nevada at Las Vegas**
ENTERED NFL: **1985**
CAREER HIGHLIGHTS: **Randall has run for more yards than any quarterback in NFL history.**
FUN FACT: **Randall enjoys golf. One of his favorite playing partners is Michael Jordan.**

RANDALL RATES:
9 of 10 for arm strength

VIKINGS

Randall has thrown for more than 27,000 yards in his career!

With Randall's rocket arm and Randy's blazing speed, the Vikings have one of the NFL's strongest long-pass threats.

PETER READ MILLER/SPORTS ILLUSTRATED

"I used to watch him back when I was in elementary school, so I know what he can do." — Randy Moss on Randall Cunningham

MINNESOTA

RANDY MOSS
WIDE RECEIVER

TOM HAUCK/ALLSPORT

RANDY FACTS

BORN: February 13, 1977, in Rand, West Virginia

HEIGHT: 6' 4"

WEIGHT: 211 pounds

COLLEGE: Marshall University

ENTERED NFL: 1998

CAREER HIGHLIGHTS: Randy set an NFL rookie record with 17 touchdown catches in 1998.

FUN FACT: Randy was twice named West Virginia's most outstanding high school basketball player.

RANDY RATES:
9 of 10 for speed

VIKINGS

"Randy is just a young kid who is a very talented athlete. He loves the game and goes out and plays."
— Randall Cunningham

In 1998, Randy took the NFL by storm with his cool catches.

The fun didn't stop there. On Thanksgiving Day in a game against the Dallas Cowboys, Randall and Randy made the Dallas defenders look like turkeys. Randall threw for 359 yards and four touchdowns in that game. Randy had three catches, and all three were long touchdowns! The Vikings won the game in a shoot-out, 46–36.

Randy was only a rookie in 1998. His success surprised a lot of people. But it was no fluke. Randy is faster and taller than almost all of the defenders who cover him. Randy was a basketball star in high school, so he can outjump defenders.

Randall has one of the strongest arms in the NFL. He can throw the ball 60 yards down the field. Combine Randy's awesome athletic ability with Randall's high-powered arm and you have two terrific touchdown teammates.

In 1998, Randall and Randy played by the Cunningham Rule all season, and the results were awesome. Randall threw for 3,704 yards and 34 touchdowns. He had only 10 interceptions in 425 pass attempts. Randall was the league's highest-rated passer!

Randy had 69 catches for 1,313 yards and 17 touchdowns. Ten of his touchdown receptions covered at least 40 yards! He was selected to play in the Pro Bowl and was named the NFL's Offensive Rookie of the Year. The rest of the league definitely noticed.

"We don't fear many players," says Detroit Lion defensive coach Larry Peccatiello. "But Randall and Randy scare us."

DALLAS COWBOYS

TROY AIKMAN
QUARTERBACK

Troy holds Cowboy records for passing attempts, completions, and yards.

PAUL JASIENSKI

TROY FACTS

Born: November 21, 1966, in West Covina, California

Height: 6' 4"

Weight: 219 pounds

College: UCLA

Entered NFL: 1989

Career Highlights: Troy holds more than 40 team passing records. He has been named to six Pro Bowls.

Fun Fact: Troy's hometown, Henryetta, Oklahoma, named a street after him.

TROY RATES:
10 of 10 for accuracy

> "If you gave me a choice to play with any quarter-back who ever played in this league, there's no one I'd pick over Troy."
> —— Michael Irvin

STEPHEN DUNN/ALLSPORT

Tuned-in teammates: Troy and Michael read each other loud and clear in practice and in games.

The Dallas Cowboys are good at keeping secrets. Their best-kept secret in recent years has been where receiver Michael Irvin was going to line up on a play. They wouldn't let anyone know until just before quarterback Troy Aikman took the snap.

Michael was all over the place in 1998. Sometimes he was near the sideline, at wide receiver. Sometimes he was in close, next to the linemen. Sometimes he even set up in the backfield, next to running back Emmitt Smith!

This confused defenses and made life much easier for Michael. "We're getting him in position to make plays," says Cowboy head coach Chan Gailey. Coach Gailey came up with the idea of moving Michael around from position to position.

Michael needed the change. He had been Troy's top pass catcher for 10 years and defenses had started ganging up on him. Opposing teams would send two defenders out to cover Michael on almost every play. Sometimes they even used three players!

"Everyone knows we're going to Michael," says Troy. "So they move people around to try to stop him."

But because Michael moved around so much in 1998, he was hard to find, much less cover. Michael had 74 catches for 1,057 yards on the season. That was almost half of Troy's passing total of 2,330 yards. Guess Troy knew where to find him!

"Troy knows the things I'm trying to do on

PLEASE TURN TO PAGE 27

MIKE DEHOOG/TDP

DALLAS COWBOYS

MICHAEL IRVIN
WIDE RECEIVER

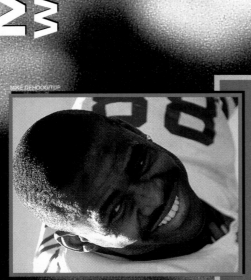

MICHAEL FACTS

BORN: March 5, 1966, in Fort Lauderdale, Florida
HEIGHT: 6' 2"
WEIGHT: 207 pounds
COLLEGE: Miami
ENTERED NFL: 1988
CAREER HIGHLIGHTS: In 1995, Michael set an NFL record for the most games with 100 or more yards. He had 11!
FUN FACT: Michael has 16 brothers and sisters.

MICHAEL RATES:
9 of 10 for hands

Troy's passes are in good hands with Michael.

> **"Without Michael, I wouldn't be such a highly rated quarterback."**
> **— Troy Aikman**

the field," Michael says. "He knows exactly where I'm going even if the play didn't dictate that."

Troy and Michael have been stressing out defenses for a long time. Michael was drafted by the Cowboys in 1988. Troy joined the team as the Number 1 pick in the 1989 draft.

Within a few years, Troy and Michael were helping the Cowboys win Super Bowls. They won three, in 1993, 1994, and 1996. One of Michael and Troy's best games was Super Bowl XXVII, in January 1993, against the Buffalo Bills. Troy threw two touchdowns to Michael just 15 seconds apart! The Cowboys cruised past Buffalo, 52–17.

In the NFC Championship Game in 1995, Troy and Michael both set Dallas playoff records. Troy threw for 380 yards. Michael caught 12 of Troy's passes for 192 yards.

"I have a great connection with Troy," Michael says. "I want to make plays for him. I want him to be confident in me."

Troy and Michael are both great players, but as people, they are very different. Troy is usually very calm during games. He doesn't yell and scream when he throws a touchdown or an interception. He just walks to the sideline to talk to the coaches.

But Michael is *always* loud. Whenever he catches a touchdown pass, he throws a party for himself in the end zone. He'll take off his helmet and wave to the crowd. Sometimes, Michael will even throw the ball to a fan!

"It's nice to get a touchdown anytime," Michael says. "That's the goal."

Michael won't tell you how he's planning to score more touchdowns. That's a secret only the Cowboys know.

VINNY TESTAVERDE
QUARTERBACK

Air-traffic controller: Vinny leads the Jets' aerial attack!

Football fans used to laugh at quarterback Vinny Testaverde and wide receiver Keyshawn Johnson of the New York Jets. They made fun of Vinny because he threw too many interceptions and his teams often lost. They thought he wasn't a winner. They laughed at Keyshawn because he likes to talk and talk . . . and talk.

In 1998, those fans stopped laughing and started cheering! Vinny and Keyshawn put up big numbers and proved to everybody that they weren't laughingstocks. They were top-notch players who could help their team win!

The so-called loser, Vinny, proved that he's a big-time winner. Before he joined the Jets in June 1998, Vinny had a 49-84-1 record as a starting quarterback for the Tampa Bay Buccaneers, Cleveland Browns, and Baltimore Ravens. But that changed quickly in New York. With Vinny as their starting quarterback, the Jets won 13 games and lost only two!

Vinny was the AFC's top-rated passer and was named to the Pro Bowl. He threw for 3,256 yards and 29 touchdowns. Vinny had only seven interceptions in 421 pass attempts.

It wasn't the result of luck, either. Vinny prepares hard during the week so that he's ready on game day. "He always knows exactly what he's looking for and where to throw the ball," says Keyshawn.

Keyshawn should know, because Vinny is usually looking for him. In 1998, the pair connected for 65 receptions, seven of them for touchdowns.

Before the 1998 season, Keyshawn was

PLEASE TURN TO PAGE 31

Ready to soar! For Vinny and Keyshawn (left), clear communication on the sidelines and in the huddle leads to success in games.

JOHN IACONO/SPORTS ILLUSTRATED

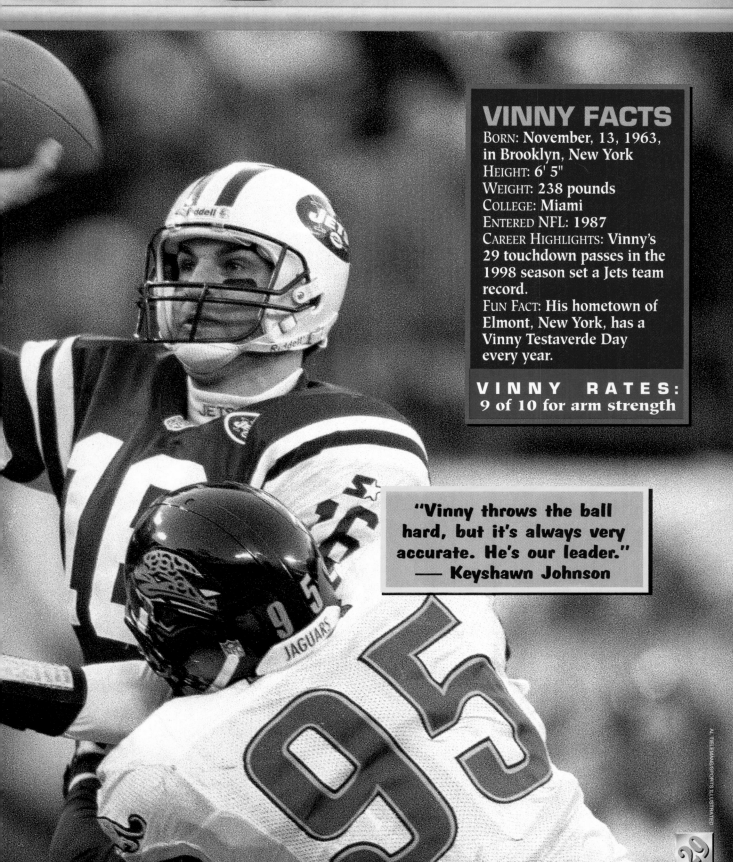

JETS

VINNY FACTS

BORN: November, 13, 1963, in Brooklyn, New York
HEIGHT: 6' 5"
WEIGHT: 238 pounds
COLLEGE: Miami
ENTERED NFL: 1987
CAREER HIGHLIGHTS: Vinny's 29 touchdown passes in the 1998 season set a Jets team record.
FUN FACT: His hometown of Elmont, New York, has a Vinny Testaverde Day every year.

VINNY RATES:
9 of 10 for arm strength

"Vinny throws the ball hard, but it's always very accurate. He's our leader."
— Keyshawn Johnson

NEW YORK

KEYSHAWN JOHNSON
WIDE RECEIVER

DAMIAN STROHMEYER/SPORTS ILLUSTRATED

Keyshawn isn't afraid to make tough catches in traffic.

KEYSHAWN FACTS

BORN: July 22, 1972, in Los Angeles, California
HEIGHT: 6' 3"
WEIGHT: 212 pounds
COLLEGE: University of Southern California (USC)
ENTERED NFL: 1996
CAREER HIGHLIGHTS: Keyshawn was the Number 1 overall draft pick in 1996. His first NFL catch was a 50-yarder against the Broncos.
FUN FACT: As a kid, Keyshawn was a ball boy for the USC football team.

KEYSHAWN RATES:
10 of 10 for size

JETS

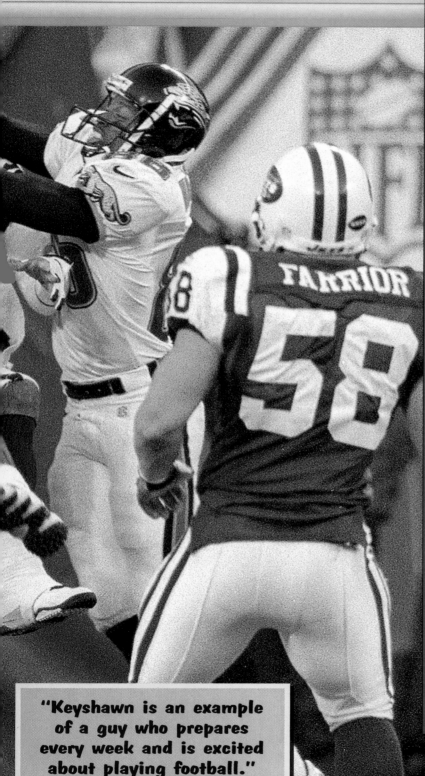

known more for his talking than his catching. He often talked about how good he was, but his statistics didn't always live up to his words. In 1998, they did. In the first game of the season, Keyshawn caught nine passes for 126 yards and two touchdowns against the San Francisco 49ers. It was just the start of what would be a great season for Keyshawn. He finished the year with 83 catches for 1,131 yards.

"Keyshawn is a guy who plays with a lot of confidence," Vinny says.

Vinny has confidence too: confidence that Keyshawn will catch passes that are thrown to him. Keyshawn is 6' 3" tall and weighs 212 pounds. That's big for a receiver. Because of his size, Keyshawn isn't afraid to catch passes in the middle of the field, where he is likely to get hit hard as soon as he does. Keyshawn isn't afraid of the defensive players who will find him there. In fact, Keyshawn isn't afraid of anything on the football field.

"Nothing's going to intimidate Keyshawn," says former Jet fullback Keith Byars. "Keyshawn wants to be the best player in the league."

Keyshawn's height also helped him catch 10 touchdown passes. When the Jets get close to the end zone, Vinny likes to throw the ball up high and let Keyshawn out-jump the smaller defensive backs for it. This simple strategy often works.

Keyshawn had plenty to jump about in his first Pro Bowl, in January 1999. He had seven catches for 87 yards and was named the game's co-MVP! "People have always told me I wouldn't be able to do certain things," Keyshawn says. "But I keep doing them."

No one is laughing anymore — except maybe his partner in success, Vinny! 🏈

> "Keyshawn is an example of a guy who prepares every week and is excited about playing football."
> — Vinny Testaverde

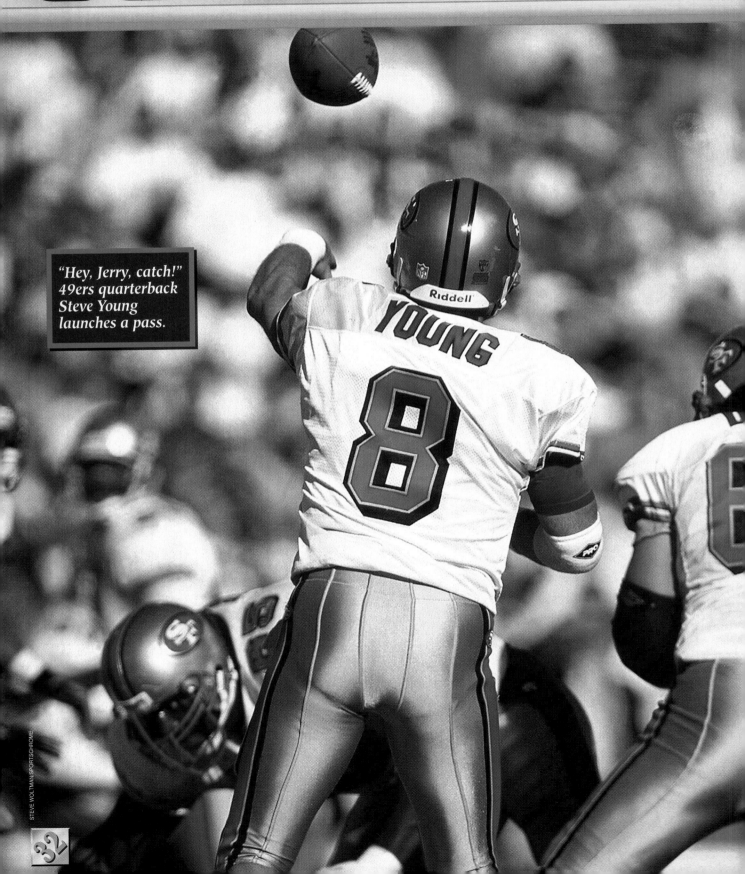

COMPLETION

"Hey, Jerry, catch!" 49ers quarterback Steve Young launches a pass.